P9-DGV-547

MAYA LIN

Architect and Artist

— PEOPLE TO KNOW —

MAYA LIN

Architect and Artist

Mary Malone

ENSLOW PUBLISHERS, INC.

44 Fadem Road P.O. Box 38
P.O. Box 699 Aldershot
Springfield, N.J. 07081 Hants GU12 6BP
U.S.A. U.K.

Library of Congress Cataloging-in-Publication Data
Malone, Mary.
    Maya Lin: architect and artist / Mary Malone.
        p. cm. —(People to know)
    Includes bibiliographical references and index.
    ISBN 0-89490-499-X
    1. Lin, Maya Ying—Juvenile literature. 2. Architects—United
States—Biography—Juvenile literature. [1. Lin, Maya Ying.
2. Architects. 3. Sculptors. 4. Chinese Americans—Biography.
5. Women—Biography.] I.Title. II. Series.
NA737.L48M35 1995
720'.92—dc20   94-5333
[B]   CIP
                                                       AC

Printed in the United States of America

10 9 8 7 6 5 4 3 2

Illustration Credits: Courtesy of Alabama Bureau of Travel and Tourism, p.
78; AP/Wide World Photos, pp. 47, 53, 91, 95; Courtesy of Charlotte/
Mecklenberg Art Commission, p. 87; Courtesy of Juniata College, p. 85;
Courtesy of Ohio University, pp. 19, 21; National Park Service, pp. 10, 37,
58, 71; Richard Howard/Time Magazine, p. 61; Ronald Reagan Library, p.
56; ©Smithsonian Institution, p. 64; UNI Photo Picture Agency, pp. 6, 42.

Cover Illustration: AP/Wide World Photos

Contents

Maya Ying Lin

"I consider myself both an artist and an architect."[1]
—*Maya Lin*

No. 1026

"Student wins war memorial contest!"[2] That was the news headlined in the newspapers on May 7, 1981. The competition for a design of a memorial to the Vietnam War veterans had been open to all citizens of the United States. But who expected a student to win? Many architects, designers, and artists, known and unknown, had entered the contest. The student who had emerged over all the other entrants was a young woman named Maya Ying Lin, Chinese-American, twenty-one years old, in her senior year at Yale University.

Maya Lin's design was described as somewhat smudged,[3] unprofessional-looking. The first time he saw it, Jan Scruggs, the young Vietnam War veteran whose brainchild the competition was, said it resembled a "big bat."[4] Other veterans wondered what qualities about the design had made such a strong impression on the judges. The college student who created it was not an architect. It was only recently that she had decided to make architecture her career. Maya Lin thought of herself as an artist first. She would receive the $20,000 prize money for first place in the competition, and the likelihood of a permanent place in any national monument-makers' Hall of Fame. She planned to use the money for further study in her chosen profession.

The group of Vietnam War veterans who sponsored the competition had recently formed themselves into a nonprofit corporation called the Vietnam Veterans Memorial Fund—VVMF. Their sole aim was to build a memorial in the nation's capital to the Vietnam War veterans. When the competition was announced in the fall of 1980, the VVMF received over 5,000 inquiries about it. By the deadline, March 31, 1981, 1,421 completed entries had been received. The entries represented a wide variety of ideas, expressed in the required two-by-four-foot panels. There were designs in the form of mounds, statues, columns, and symbols of war. The names on the entries were removed from sight, and numbers assigned to them. The bulky packages had to be stored in an airplane hangar at Andrews Air Force base outside Washington. Set up for display, they covered over a mile of space. Late in April, they were ready to be judged. The panel of judges, a group of eminent architects and landscape designers, had one week to decide the winner.

The VVMF had hoped for a great memorial to come from the design competition. They really had no preconceived idea of what they wanted in a memorial except for one overriding feature. The memorial had to have on it the names of the almost 58,000 American Vietnam War soldiers killed or missing in action. Other than that, the VVMF entrusted their project to the expert knowledge of the renowned panel of judges who knew what art was all about. Ideally, as one newspaper critic, Wolf Von Eckhardt, said, long before the competition was officially announced, great monuments are "simply powerful ideas translated into a powerful response."[5] This was a prophetic statement, uncannily descriptive of the winning design.

Although much of the public believed that holding a competition for a memorial design was something new, that was not the case. The VVMF had chosen an open competition, instead of selecting an architect themselves, because they believed it would be both more democratic and more likely to increase public support. But competitions for the design of memorials have been held throughout American history. That's how the White House came into existence. A design competition in 1792 was won by Irish-born James Hoban for his classic, Grecian-inspired design. The Washington Monument, a landmark in the capital, also came from a design

The Vietnam Veterans Memorial after its completion. At the start, no one had any preconceived ideas of how it might look.

competition, won by Robert Mills in 1833, although his design was later altered. Maya Lin was following an honored tradition by submitting, in open competition, her design for a national monument. The surprising outcome was that although she was very young, without any experience as an architect, her design turned out to be the "powerful idea" the judges recognized.

The judges had begun their huge task by narrowing the field of 1,421 entries to thirty-nine finalists. They then eliminated all but eighteen. They kept going back to one design, No. 1026. That design not only impressed them, it "haunted" them.[6] Although it did not look as polished as some of the other designs by professional architects, it was strangely compelling. Two long black marble walls (each design was accompanied by a written explanation) delved into the earth, then rose and met at an angle. Together they resembled the two sides of a triangle. The walls would have on them the names of the 58,000 soldiers killed or missing in action in Vietnam.

Simple and direct though it was, No. 1026 seemed to the judges to have fulfilled all the regulations of the competition in a unique and unconventional way. Especially noted was the memorial's harmony with its location, the hallowed ground of Constitution Gardens on the Mall, not far from the Capitol. It would lie between the two greatest monuments in the city, the

Lincoln Memorial to the west, the Washington Monument to the east.

At the end of the week, No. 1026 was unanimously awarded first place. Before that, the judges went back and voted again just to make sure they all agreed. "Of all the proposals submitted," they said, "this most clearly meets the spirit and formal requirements of the program. It is contemplative and reflective. It is superbly harmonious with its site."[7]

When it was revealed that the winner was a "dark horse," a surprise choice, the news flashed across the country. Maya Lin became a celebrity. She was interviewed, photographed, seen on television. Her life story—short as it was—was published in many newspapers. Praise and congratulations poured in, not only for the young designer, but for the VVMF too. Maya Lin was described by B. Drummond Ayres in *The New York Times* as "pleased, enjoying herself."[8] When her design was made public, it was praised by many art critics. One said that the judges "must have felt a sense of excitement and discovery"[9] when they came upon Lin's design and selected it as the best of all the entries in the largest design competition ever held in the United States.

Good feeling about the award and the winner prevailed for some time. But as the result of the competition received more publicity, stirrings of dissent began to arise. Many people, some of them prominent, did not like the design at all and spoke out against it. It

12

may have been unique and unconventional, as the judges believed, but it was not what had been expected. It was quite a departure from the usual concept of a memorial. People remembered what the great monuments of the past looked like—the Cenotaph in London, for example, a huge monument built to honor those (in this case, British soldiers killed in war) whose bodies were missing or buried elsewhere. In days gone by, when men wore hats, they raised them whenever they passed the Cenotaph.[10] Another famous traditional-style monument is in Arlington National Cemetery in Washington, D.C. It is a sculpture of six United States marines raising the American flag on Iwo Jima during World War II.

A lot of Vietnam War veterans across the country—those outside the Washington-based VVMF—were upset by Maya Lin's design. They hadn't been consulted, and they were outraged by the fact that someone who knew nothing about the Vietnam War had designed a memorial for their comrades. A writer for *The Washington Post* commented that "a woman who was four years old when the first bodies came home, had designed a national memorial to be built on the Mall."[11] Other people found it ironic that an Asian-American woman had designed a memorial to an American military action in Southeast Asia. However, the American public, on the whole, displayed no prejudice regarding that coincidence. The fact that Maya Lin's

13

family so opposed communism that they left China for America emphasizes ideology rather than race.

The criticism turned into a controversy between those who praised the design as a fine example of modern art and those who preferred the older, more familiar style.

Coming after the elation of winning the competition's award, the criticism about her design shocked Lin. As time went on, it changed her outlook. At the age of twenty-one, no longer sheltered in a college atmosphere, she was to learn a great deal—about people, politics, and compromises.

"If you present me with a problem and I like it and think I can work with it, I'll do it." [1]—*Maya Lin*

The Beginning

Maya Lin's story began in China, many years before she was born. Her family on both sides included talented people. The Lins and the Changs—her mother's forebears—belonged to the elite class. They were doctors, lawyers, artists, scholars. They joined the Nationalist party of Sun Yat-sen, who was credited with overthrowing the last repressive Chinese dynasty in 1911. After that, for some years, China had a more open, democratic society.

In 1921, Maya Lin's grandfather, Lin Chang-min, a lawyer, was sent by the Chinese government to Europe as director of his country's delegation to the League of Nations. Although that attempt by many nations to promote peace failed, it was eventually succeeded in 1946 by the present United Nations. Mr. Lin's seventeen-year-old daughter, Lin Hui-yin, accompanied her father.[2] She was a beautiful, intelligent young woman who made many friends, especially in London where she met well-known writers and poets. When the Lins returned to China, she married, according to her father's wishes, Liang Si-chang, who was an architectural historian. The couple traveled to the United States to complete their education at the University of Pennsylvania. While in America, the young woman who would become Maya Lin's aunt enrolled for a term at Yale University, where she studied the architecture of stage design. Later, with her husband in China, she worked on architectural history. The two traveled throughout the country, locating and saving many of the old, historic buildings.

Maya's father, Henry Huan Lin, was the younger brother of Lin Hui-yin. He has said that his daughter Maya resembles her. Like his sister, he said, "Maya is very emotional, very sensitive."[3] Henry Lin added that all the female Lins were strong, independent women. He himself was an artist in ceramics, a collector also of ancient porcelain pieces.

Several years after Sun Yat-sen's time, during the 1920s and 1930s, China was unsettled politically by warring factions. The Nationalists were opposed by an ever-growing Communist party, which was aided by the Soviet Union. Fighting continued during and after World War II. General Chiang Kai-shek, who led the

Nationalists, was finally defeated in 1949 and had to flee to the island of Taiwan, which had been occupied by Japan and ceded back to China by the Japanese after the war. There the Nationalists established the Republic of China in Taiwan.

People still in mainland China who had belonged to the Nationalist party were in danger from the Chinese Communist forces. Many who could, like Maya Lin's parents, escaped during the late 1940's, and some of them came to the United States.

After he arrived in America, Henry Lin, through his excellent educational qualifications, obtained a position at Ohio University in Athens, Ohio. He met Maya's mother, Julia Chang, sometime afterward. The daughter of a physician, Julia had been smuggled out of China by her relatives. She was a teenager at the time she left, with nothing but a hundred dollar bill pinned to her coat lining.[4] After she landed in the United States, the young woman was helped by friends of the Chinese Nationalist party. They enrolled her at Smith College in Northampton, Massachusetts, where she had been granted a scholarship.

She graduated from Smith in 1951 and soon thereafter met Henry Lin. They were married and settled in Athens, Ohio, where both of them were on the faculty of Ohio University for many years. The Lins' two children were born in Athens, first a son, Tan, and three years later, Maya, on October 5, 1959. Her name came from the Hindu goddess, the mother of Buddha, but more personally, it was also the name of a friend of Julia Chang's at Smith College, "a beautiful Indian girl."[5] Maya's Chinese middle name, Ying, can be translated as "precious stone."

At Ohio University, Julia Lin taught Oriental and English literature. She also wrote poetry and had books published on the subject of Chinese poetry. Henry Lin rose to the position of professor of art at the university and, in time, became dean of the department of fine arts.

Maya and her brother were raised as "faculty brats,"[6] the name given to the children of the university's faculty. The college atmosphere of Athens, a town of some 22,000 residents, characterized the area. According to the Lins' daughter, Athens was a "perfect" place to grow up. "You could leave your keys in your car, leave your door unlocked."[7]

Ideal as all this was, however, Maya Lin has admitted that she never felt really at home in Athens. In part, that was because her parents did not consider Athens their real home. "Their home was gone," Maya said.[8] She and her brother, who were part of an extremely close-knit family, reflected their parents' feeling of being strangers in a strange land. But with their varied artistic talents, they were all happily and creatively occupied in a house cluttered with books and art materials. Art and literature were part of the Lins' daily life.

As one writer said, "Although Maya Lin is an

18

Maya Lin grew up as a "faculty brat" of Ohio University in Athens, Ohio. Her parents both taught at the school.

American girl from the Midwest, she is Chinese in her bones."[9]

Their parents' interests were shared by the Lin children. Maya watched her father at his pottery wheel and as a small child often begged him to let her fire and "throw" a bowl. As Tan grew up, his interest was concentrated on poetry, and like his mother, he became a poet.

Maya spent a lot of time in her room, constructing little villages of paper or leftover materials from her father's studio. As she grew older, she worked on ceramics, sculpture, silversmithing. That was her way of expressing creative ideas, which her mother and brother did in poetry. Outdoors, she loved to go bird-watching and to wander in the woods near her home.

Besides artistic pursuits, the Lin family had a strong interest in nature and the environment. The natural world was not far away from home, which was called by one writer, "a glass-walled house in the woods."[10] That feeling for the environment would motivate Maya Lin when she was designing buildings later on. She was always site-oriented,[11] as she said, in her consideration for keeping intact the natural setting of a planned structure. Phil McCombs, a writer for *The Washington Post*, quotes from Lin Yutang, a well-known Chinese author (no relation to Maya Lin) who said, "The best architecture is that which loses itself in the natural landscape and becomes one with it, belongs to it."[12]

Athens, Ohio was Maya Lin's hometown, but she never really felt "at home" there.

Both Maya and her brother preferred reading to watching television. As a child, Maya liked stories about dwarfs and elves and magical lands, such as *The Lion, the Witch and the Wardrobe* by C. S. Lewis and *The Hobbit* by J. R. R. Tolkien. Later on, she enjoyed the tales of Greek mythology. With her brother, she played chess and solved puzzles involving problems in logic. Photography was a strong interest for her.

The Lin children had freedom to do the things they liked. Neither parent enforced strict discipline, no doubt because responsibility had been instilled early in the youngsters. They studied and worked at their own pace. "My parents brought us up to decide what we wanted to do, where we wanted to study," Maya said. "They never forced us to do anything. We always had a choice."[13]

When she started high school, Maya found that her interests were not like those of most of her classmates. She said that "everyone was worried about getting A's, B's, and C's. I really thought it was kind of stupid. High school was really miserable. I disliked talking to people. Socially, I kind of ignored the whole scene. Boys and girls all taking themselves so seriously. The girls into make-up. It was just not at all my idea of a life, of anything interesting."[14]

Maya was more interested in figuring a problem in trigonometry than in being one of the crowd. Although she has said, jokingly, "I guess you could say I was somewhat of a nerd,"[15] she also said frankly that she was not happy in high school. Being of an independent nature does not always make for popularity with one's peers.

On the outside, Maya did, in some ways, appear as a typical high school student. She dressed like all the others in school—jeans, t-shirts, and sneakers. She wore her hair long, hanging down her back. Also, like many of her contemporaries, she worked at a local McDonald's. "It was the only way to earn some money," she said.[16]

She was an excellent student, of course. Math was her favorite subject. She read books on a college level. She took some college courses while still in high school and had no trouble being accepted by the college of her choice—Yale in New Haven, Connecticut. Her brother had decided on Columbia University in New York City. Maya chose Yale because, as she said, it was "academically challenging,"[17] Yale may very well have chosen her not only for her high academic standing— she was co-valedictorian of her graduating class—but also for her artistic talent and her family background. Whatever it was that drew Maya Lin and Yale University together, it was a fortunate happening for both of them, as later events would prove.

"I'm a true-blue Yalie."[1]—*Maya Lin*

3

The University

Almost from the beginning, Maya Lin felt at home in Yale. It was "the first place where I felt comfortable,"[2] she said. Her creativity as well as her love of learning were recognized early by her teachers. She found that the university atmosphere was congenial, a place where students and professors from all over the world came together. Even after graduation, she often returned to Yale.

As an undergraduate, she lived in a campus residence hall (dormitory) with a roommate, Liz Perry, who became a good friend. With other friends, Lin often went roller-skating for relaxation. Her studies for the first two undergraduate years were liberal-arts-related—literature, philosophy, science. Of the electives possible, Lin chose photography. She still read a great deal and, like many other students, pondered the significance of life and death, the meaning of existence.

Although she was not quite the loner of her high school days, Lin often went on solitary walks through the streets of New Haven. Not long after she arrived at Yale, she discovered the Grove Street cemetery on one of her walks, right in the heart of the city. She returned to it whenever she wanted a quiet time by herself. "There's something peaceful about it," she said. "You feel removed. You feel you're in their world…the world of the dead."[3] Death to her then was still an abstract idea—something not real. She thought a lot about it, however, as she strolled through the cemetery. "I've always been intrigued with death," she explained, "and man's reaction to it."[4] She noted the ways the dead are remembered—the memorials, statues, epitaphs on the headstones. "Everybody knows I'm morbid,"[5] she said lightly, in explanation of her fascination with the subject. Her friends, however, would deny that she was morbid. They described her as "artistic, emotional, and sensitive."[6]

Yale University, besides its undergraduate college, includes many schools of special, advanced study. These include medicine, law, drama, and architecture. After the general academic studies of their first two years, students select a major field, which is concentrated on for the remaining two years. Sometimes after graduation with a bachelor's degree, they enroll in the graduate school of their specialty for advanced study and a master's degree.

How Lin decided on architecture as her choice seemed offhand, as she explained it. She was sitting in the college library one day, staring up at the ceiling, "at all the lines and painting on it...and suddenly, I decided I was going to be an architect. Just like that."[7] Although it might appear to be a hasty decision, it really wasn't. All her life, Lin had been influenced by her family's artistic background. Her aunt, Lin Hui-yin, was part of it. Her father was an artist, her mother a poet. Designing things—model towns, ceramics, sculptures—came from Lin's own interest in artistic creation. She considered herself an artist, and architecture was art on a large scale.

In her junior year of college, Lin went with a group of other Yale students to Europe to study for a semester. She attended Copenhagen University in Denmark. Enrolled in courses in city planning and landscape design, she enjoyed walking around the section of Copenhagen known as Norrebro. One of her assignments was to study that area, with its well-laid-out residential avenues and a beautiful, parklike cemetery. She noted that the cemetery was a place where people could go to enjoy the natural beauty of the surroundings. Other such cemeteries in other countries in Europe impressed Lin in the same way. Some of them—in Paris and in London—besides being the burial places of famous people, attracted visitors for other reasons.

"European countries make their graveyards into living gardens,"[8] Lin said. People would go to them for relaxation in the midst of teeming cities. On Sundays, parents might bring their children along to stroll and enjoy seeing the trees and flowers.

Many contemporary city planners consider that cemeteries are an essential "green space" for a balanced urban environment. In some of them, jogging, biking, and hiking paths have been included in the plans, as well as picnic and other recreational areas.

While in Denmark, Lin took trips to many famous sites and buildings in different European countries, the very old structures as well as the new. No aspiring architect would neglect seeing the architecture of the early Greeks, which in its classic, balanced proportions has influenced western architecture for over two thousand years. Lin visited the buildings of the Acropolis in Athens where the Parthenon stands, the ancient temple dedicated to the goddess Athena. She saw the palace of Knossos on the island of Crete, a surviving reminder of the architecture of the Bronze Age of over four thousand years ago.

She also saw examples of modern architecture in Europe, buildings designed by two great architects of the modern style—Mies Van Der Rohe and Walter Gropius. Both of these famous men emigrated to the United States from Germany in the 1930s before the Nazis took control of their country. Their ideas greatly influenced the study of architecture in the American universities, especially Yale and Harvard.

While she was in Denmark, Lin was surprised to learn that ethnic differences were still not as acceptable there as in the United States. One day when she boarded a streetcar and sat down, everybody near her rose and sat somewhere else.[9] It was the first time Lin was made aware that her Asian appearance might disturb people. The experience made her appreciate America and say, sometime later, to Lilly Wei, who interviewed her for *Art in America*, that although she could be identified as Chinese-American, if she had to she would choose American. "I don't have an allegiance to any country but this one; it is my home…still a place where a lot can get done. This is a country that allows you the freedom to do what you can."[10]

Lin returned to Yale ready to begin her last college year. She would turn twenty-one in October of 1980. After that, graduation would be the big event to anticipate. Who could have predicted that something many times more momentous than her graduation would occur in the coming year and change the course of her life?

"I liked my idea. That's why I entered the contest." [1]

—Maya Lin

The Competition

In November 1980, Professor Andrus Burr of Yale University gave his senior architecture students a special assignment. It was to design a memorial for the recently announced Vietnam War veterans' competition.

This design competition was the second step in the VVMF's Operation Memorial. The first—to obtain the land—was accomplished. The dream of Jan Scruggs, obsessed with the determination to commemorate his fellow veterans, was going to become reality.

Scruggs had served as an infantryman in the war and had seen half of his company killed. That was something he could never forget. He was wounded himself and returned from Vietnam with shrapnel still in his legs.

Back home in Washington, D.C., Scruggs was appalled by the reaction of the public to the returning veterans. There were no parades or public ceremonies for them, just coldness and hostility. Bitterness over the United States' involvement in the conflict seemed to be transferred to the soldiers who had served in that unpopular war. Scruggs was bothered most by the lack of recognition for the sacrifice of so many lives. After brooding about it for several years, he decided that if anything was to be done, he himself would have to do it. One day he announced to his wife, "I'm going to build a memorial to all the guys who served in Vietnam. It'll have the name of everyone killed."[2]

Jan Scruggs believed that America needed such a memorial: recognition for the veterans, reconciliation for the people. He began his crusade alone. Very little attention was paid to his quest for contributions until a local television station gave him a small spot on its nightly news program. That attracted two prominent lawyers in Washington, Vietnam veterans also—John Wheeler and Robert Doubek. With Jan Scruggs, they formed the nonprofit corporation to carry on the drive, and the campaign took off.

Through the untiring efforts of the VVMF leaders, joined in time by many volunteers, the money coming in increased dramatically. Before the drive was over, more than 275,000 Americans responded to the VVMF campaign with contributions in small denominations as well as large. The families and relatives of the Vietnam veterans were especially anxious to help the cause and gave generously according to their means. Eventually the entire seven million dollars needed to build the memorial came from the people. It "did not cost the government a dime,"[3] one journalist wrote. That was the way the VVMF wanted it. In order to keep their independence from bureaucratic red tape and delays, they had decided not to accept any government money for the memorial.

The VVMF made a timetable for their plan. It was brief:

1980—Obtain land for the memorial.

1981—Select a design and finish fund-raising.

1982—Complete construction; conduct
dedication on Veterans Day.

A lot of people told the VVMF that their timetable was impossible. No memorial had ever been built in three years. But the VVMF was determined to do it. First they lobbied Congress, whose approval was needed for building the memorial on a two-acre tract of land on the Mall. In the heart of Washington, D.C., this land was difficult to wrest from Congressional control. Known as Constitution Gardens, it had been developed from a former swamp by a well-known landscape architect, Henry Arnold. That was in 1976, to commemorate in the bicentennial year the fifty-six signers of the Declaration of Independence. Close to the Capitol, Constitution Gardens was a parklike setting with beautiful vistas.

Congress delayed and objected and suggested other spots outside the city. The VVMF refused any location other than Constitution Gardens. Eventually, Congress gave in and granted approval.

Next came the selection of a design for the memorial. The open competition chosen by the VVMF would help publicize the campaign. Jan Scruggs and his codirectors who had appointed the blue-ribbon panel of architects and landscape designers to judge the entries, hoped for a design with a "powerful idea."[4]

In the guidelines the VVMF sent out to all those who inquired about the competition, there were other objectives named besides Jan Scruggs's. His—to have the names of all the war dead on the memorial—was the one specific requirement listed. The others were more general. The memorial should be in harmony with its location. That was prompted by John Wheeler's hope for a "landscape solution,"[5] a horizontal structure in a garden setting. Although this was mentioned, the VVMF would not exclude any ideas or forms—if they were powerful enough. Robert Doubek's hope was for a monument that would "recognize and honor those who served and died...to begin a healing process."[6]

After the competition got under way in the autumn of 1980 and the deadline—four months away—settled, the VVMF members had only to wait for the great design they hoped would emerge. They looked forward to seeing a design that would put into stone and marble their resolve to give the Vietnam War veterans the respect and honor that was long overdue.

At Yale University, the announcement of the competition came at an appropriate time. Professor Burr's class had just completed a seminar on funerary architecture, in which they had studied memorials and monuments for the dead. Outstanding war memorials in France built for the slain soldiers of World War I were especially noted. Most of those were erected where the great battles had raged—the Somme, Ypres, the Meuse Argonne. They were awesome structures, rising over the thousands of graves of the soldiers killed there.

The subject of war memorials interested at least one student in Professor Burr's class. Maya Lin thought that creating a design for a modern war memorial was a "great idea."[7] However, she knew very little about the Vietnam War and the United States' involvement in it. The struggle in Southeast Asia that had torn this country apart had been over for some years. Lin was a small child when the fiercest battles raged in Vietnam. There were demonstrations against the war at Ohio University, as well as at many other American college campuses. When that happened in Athens, Maya Lin was kept inside. It wasn't until much later that she understood the significance of the riots and demonstrations. Since the war ended, she had not read any books about it or seen any of the films which depicted the violence and bloodshed. She said once, "I hate war. All wars."[8]

The United States' involvement in Vietnam began in 1959 in a limited way, with only military advisers sent to help South Vietnam. The country of Vietnam had been partitioned, when the French, who had ruled it since 1885, were defeated by Communist forces. North Vietnam was ruled by a Communist government, supported by China and the Soviet Union in its attempt to take over South Vietnam. The South Vietnamese government was anti-Communist and pro-American. The United States' commitment to South Vietnam was explained by General William C. Westmoreland, who would become the commander of the American forces in Vietnam. It was "the desire of a strong nation to help an aspiring nation achieve independence."[9]

By 1963, 16,000 American combat troops had been sent to Vietnam. The numbers escalated until by the war's end, ten years later, 850,000 soldiers had served in the desperate cause. The guerrilla warfare waged by the North Vietnamese and their sympathizers from the South was never stopped. In 1973, by an agreement known as the Paris Accords, the American involvement in the war in Vietnam was ended, and the troops began to withdraw. The agreement was that the people of South Vietnam would decide on their own future government. But two years after the cease-fire, the North Vietnamese overran South Vietnam, and all remaining United States personnel were evacuated, along with many South Vietnamese refugees. In 1976, the two

sections of Vietnam were unified, and the country became known as the Socialist Republic of Vietnam.

The Vietnam War's toll was 58,000 American soldiers killed or missing in action and 300,000 wounded; over two million men and women served time in Vietnam in noncombat roles. In Vietnam, millions of civilians were killed, wounded, uprooted from their homes, or exposed to deadly chemicals. Their children were orphaned. Agent Orange, a powerful defoliant meant to destroy plant life, was sprayed over many sections of the land by the United States military. Its effects are still felt, not only by the Vietnamese but also by the American soldiers who were exposed to it.

Even during the competition, Maya Lin did not read about the Vietnam War. She did not want to be influenced by politics. But she did read a great deal about memorials and their meaning. In thinking about a memorial dedicated to the Vietnam War veterans, she said, "I felt a memorial should be honest about the reality of war, and be for the people who gave their lives."[10] Remembrance, healing, reconciliation—all those should be represented in the memorial. How? Lin read and reread the guidelines the VVMF had issued. Besides the definite requirement of having the names of those killed in the war inscribed on the monument, there was another condition that had great meaning for Lin. The memorial should be in harmony with its site—between the monuments that were Washington landmarks. The

Lincoln Memorial itself symbolized reconciliation between North and South after the Civil War.

What form should her design take? Lin still had no idea. But soon she knew she had to see the site.

After the Thanksgiving recess, Lin and several of her fellow students met at Constitution Gardens in Washington, D.C. She saw at once that the VVMF was right. This beautiful landscape definitely called for a memorial in harmony with it. She walked all over the site and took many photographs: the sloping ground, the background trees, the glistening monuments in the distance. It was a quiet, peaceful place. After a half hour, as she explained later, "The design sort of popped into my head. I wanted some sort of journey into the earth."[11] A rift in the earth was what she visualized, "with the memorial going into the ground, then emerging from it, symbolizing death and calling for remembrance."[12] She said that she "thought about what death is and what a loss is—a sharp pain that lessens with time but can never quite heal over. A scar. The idea occurred to me there on the site."[13]

Lin returned to Yale, and, as she said, "I sketched the idea and worked it up in clay. It seemed almost too simple. Then I recalled…all the names of those killed and missing in action must be part of the memorial…the names would become the memorial. There was no need to embellish."[14] The final result of her work was a pastel sketch of two black walls going into, then rising from the

The Lincoln Memorial, in Washington, D.C. After the Civil War, this monument had symbolized reconciliation between North and South.

earth, against a background of trees and grass. Lin showed it to her classmates and asked for reactions from them and Professor Burr. The students wondered why the walls of the memorial were not white. Lin said that the black marble would give more reflection to the names. Professor Burr suggested that the two walls on the design should come together to form an angle. Lin agreed with this and also with her teacher's suggestion that the names on the wall should be arranged chronologically by the date of death, not alphabetically. She saw the logic of that and also how the names could come together to indicate the war's beginning and end. "The time sequence, which has the dates of the first and last deaths meeting at the intersection of these walls, is the essence of the design,"[15] she told the VVMF later. Lin revised her design and mailed it to Washington. She was the only student in her class who submitted an entry in the competition. Even as she sent it off, however, she herself had some doubts about it. Although she liked it, she felt that her design couldn't win. "It was too different, too strange,"[16] she said. Professor Burr thought it was "too strong,"[17] and graded it B but urged her to send it in anyway.

A month later, Lin was sitting in class when her roommate appeared at the door and passed a note to her. Washington had called, asking for Maya Lin. They would call again in fifteen minutes. Lin hurried to her room in time to get the second call. It was from Colonel

Don Schaet, a staff member of the VVMF. "Don't get excited," he told Lin. "And please don't tell anyone about this call. We're coming up to talk to you."[18]

Such a message would naturally make one wonder. Did it mean the possibility of an award—a minor one, maybe honorable mention? Lin waited. Later that day, three VVMF staff members arrived at Yale and met her in the dormitory. Don Schaet, who was a retired Marine Corps colonel, started off by explaining how important the proposed memorial was. Lin listened. One of the other visitors said, "Come on. Tell her." Shaet nodded. "All right," he said. "You've won. First prize."[19]

If they expected to see Maya Lin jump up and down and scream with joy, they were disappointed. She said nothing, showed no emotion. Her very first feeling, she said later, was disbelief.[20] This could not be happening to her.

After the first reaction, she listened attentively to Colonel Schaet. She heard him ask if she could get down to Washington soon for a press conference. Lin could, the very next day. Although it was final exam time, she would postpone a scheduled exam. After the visitors left, she tried to convince herself that she had really won first prize. That evening, she called her parents to tell them the news. Then she tried to sleep. On the following day, she flew to Washington alone. At the VVMF headquarters, she met the sponsors of the competition. They saw a young woman who looked even younger than twenty-one. She was not much different in appearance from the teenager who had entered Yale as a freshman—small, slight, five feet three inches tall, and ninety pounds. She was not wearing makeup, and her long black hair was still halfway down her back. The VVMF people liked what they saw, and they applauded as she walked in. Lin smiled then. She began to believe what was happening. She had really won.

"If you want to change something, reconvene the jury."[1]
—*Maya Lin*

Controversy

At the first press conference held by the VVMF after the competition award, a model of the winning design was on view. Maya Lin explained it to the journalists present. She said the memorial would consist of two long walls, each over two hundred feet long, coming together to form an angle somewhat like a triangle. Beginning underground and rising to a height of ten feet, the walls would meet at the apex of the triangle. They would be inscribed with the names of the nearly 58,000 Americans confirmed dead in the Vietnam War.

As Lin and Professor Burr had decided, the names would be in chronological, not alphabetical, order, grouped according to the dates of death. She explained the reason for that at the press conference. An alphabetical arrangement would put the same names

Maya Lin shows her winning design in the Vietnam Veterans Memorial competition. It was not long before controversy arose surrounding the design.

together. (As she learned afterward, there were over six hundred Smiths among the casualties, and sixteen named James Jones.) That arrangement would make the memorial look "like a telephone book engraved in granite."[2] The chronological order would draw together the names of comrades killed at the same time, often in the same battle. Lin had already, in her first talks with the VVMF, convinced them that this idea for listing the names was the logical one.

In addition, Lin had to explain why the memorial should be black marble, instead of white, like most of the other memorials in Washington. Besides reflecting the names better, black marble could be polished to give a mirrorlike image of the Mall and the people looking at the names. The effect would be as if people and the names came together. To a writer who interviewed her later, Lin said that "the color black is a lot more peaceful and gentle than white. White marble may be very beautiful, but you can't read anything on it."[3]

The newspapers published all this, and Lin received a great deal of publicity. Interviewed several times, she was forthcoming and cooperative, and gave out quite a few details about her life and family. She was described by Jonathan Coleman in *Time* as "shy, yet affable, serious but quick to smile, and full of energy."[4] As time went on, however, Lin would not welcome the continued publicity, especially from the merely curious. "Her private life is something she guards fiercely,"[5] Coleman commented later.

After the VVMF announcement of the award, Lin's father in Athens, Ohio, was asked what he thought of his daughter's winning design. He described it as "simple, yet very direct,"[6] somewhat Chinese, he believed, in that her family culture might be said to show in her work. Although in later years, Lin conceded that her artistic outlook was "distinctly Asian,"[7] she said now, "I don't speak or write Chinese,"[8] and her mother commented that "Maya is so modern in so many ways. She considers herself much more American than Chinese."[9] Mrs. Lin's influence was noted when her daughter described the design that won the judges' admiration as "visual poetry"[10] and later said that the Wall (as the memorial became known) "could be read like an epic Greek poem."[11]

After the description of the design was made public, however, differences of opinion about it arose. Not everybody admired the favorite of the judges and the art "elite." The criticism grew and soon a controversy began—between those who favored modern art, as Maya Lin's design was labeled, and those who disliked it. Modern art is often abstract, difficult to understand. It portrays ideas and impressions, not reality. The traditional style depicts scenes and portraits as they might be in life, or as they are "represented."

The opponents of Maya Lin's design wanted a

traditional monument, in keeping with the familiar ones positioned around Washington—statues of famous figures, heroes on horseback, and the like. A stark, unadorned set of walls with names instead of symbols was abstract to many people.

The memorial-to-be was called "unheroic" because it would be partly below ground level; a "black gash of shame"; a "degrading ditch"; a "wailing wall for Vietnam War protesters";[12] and more. The architecture critic of a leading newspaper said, "The so-called memorial is bizarre, neither a building nor sculpture."[13]

Maya Lin, upset by the criticism, said scathingly, "Modern art makes a lot of people nervous."[14] She hoped people would not close their minds about the memorial before they saw it completed. In fact, one of the judges of the competition had foreseen the negative reaction. He said that "many people would not understand the design until they experienced it."[15] Maya Lin herself never lost faith in the integrity of her work. She was sure her design would result in the right kind of memorial for those who had sacrificed their lives as well as for those who mourned them.

Jan Scruggs and his fellow directors of the VVMF, when they first looked at the design, did not quite know what to say. They had listened to the judges' description of the winning entry. Maya Lin, the experts told them, had created "an eloquent place where the simple setting of earth, sky and remembered names" come together.[16]

45

The design would result in a "monument for our times."[17] It would be harmonious with its site, "entering the earth rather than piercing the sky."[18] The VVMF listened, and agreed—but still—they wondered.

Jan Scruggs kept staring at this strange thing that his organization had brought into existence. At first it seemed to him a weird design.[19] But as he stood silently, brooding, he saw that those massive walls, longer than a football field, when built would contain the 58,000 names, all of them. He was satisfied. "It's a great memorial," he said.[20]

John Wheeler and Robert Doubek, too, had second thoughts the longer they looked at the design. "I was surprised," Doubek recalled. "We were silent for a moment. But when we understood...the genius of the simple concept, it took effect on us. We embraced and congratulated each other. We were thrilled."[21]

When the opponents of the design finally realized that they could not replace it with another, they demanded changes or additions to it. At the very least, they wanted a statue and a flag. Maya Lin protested. She was against any additions to the memorial. The names were enough. "I'll be stubborn about that," she said,[22] and she was. She resisted the idea of a flag being placed on the memorial because it was her belief that, as the guidelines of the competition read, the memorial should avoid making a political statement. Besides, as she said, a flag would make the site "look like a golf green."[23]

Jan Scruggs and Maya Lin standing before the names on the Wall.
At first Scruggs was skeptical about Lin's design, but soon called it
"a great memorial."

The opposition to the design was keeping the VVMF from completing the final step of their timetable. Even worse, it might prevent the memorial from ever getting built. The secretary of the interior, whose department included the National Park Service and whose permission was necessary before construction could be started, sided with those against the design. Finally, realizing that their whole plan was in danger, the VVMF directors decided that a compromise would have to be made. They were willing to add a statue and a flag, but not on the memorial itself. The secretary of the interior and other influential opponents of Maya Lin's design accepted the compromise. Then the VVMF hired a sculptor to create a statue. Their choice was Frederick Hart, who had won third place in the design competition. Hart began his work on a realistic statue of three servicemen in the Vietnam War. It was to be ready for dedication in 1984.

However, the VVMF had not consulted Maya Lin about their action. When she heard of it, she was angry, and made her feelings known. She said she had been treated like a child,[24] overlooked on a matter that was vital to "her" memorial. She called the placing of a statue at the memorial like "drawing mustaches on other people's portraits."[25]

Jan Scruggs, whose driving motive had always been to get the 58,000 names on the memorial, said that the compromise was "the only way to get Maya Lin's piece built."[26] He added that the way it would be done would not detract from her design. The Fine Arts Commission and many well-known architects who were on Maya Lin's side agreed that the memorial design itself should not be compromised. The VVMF was instructed to make sure that the proposed statue and flag would be placed at a considerable distance from the memorial. The VVMF followed through on that.

Lin had also disagreed at first with the VVMF about placing an inscription on the Wall. The VVMF wanted the inscription to honor *all* the Vietnam veterans. Lin firmly believed that nothing should be on the memorial but the names of those killed in the war. But the VVMF pointed out that the 2.7 million men and women who had served in Vietnam over the course of the war deserved some recognition. As it was impossible to have all those names on the memorial, an inscription would satisfy the VVMF's wish to honor them. Lin then agreed, and an inscription in two parts—a prologue and an epilogue—was placed at the Wall's beginning and end. It reminds visitors to remember the courage and dedication of all those who served in the war.

The VVMF had originally wanted the inscription to be in large gilt letters. Kent Cooper, an architect from the firm Lin worked with on the project, rejected that idea. "No word, no letter should be more noticeable than any name," he said.[27] And so the final inscription did not overshadow the names. Maya Lin remained true to her belief that nothing should go on the face of the memorial except the names. She refused to have her own name there. Instead, it is behind the memorial, out of public view, along with the names of the other people who were instrumental in building the Wall.

"It does not glorify the war or make an antiwar statement."[1]
—*Maya Lin*

A Monument
for Our Times

After Maya Lin graduated from Yale with a bachelor of arts degree, she moved to Washington, D.C. She lived with two designer friends from Yale in an old ramshackle row house on Capitol Hill. In her spare time, she helped her friends remodel the house.

Starting that summer of 1981, she worked as a consultant with the architectural firm the VVMF had engaged to develop the Vietnam memorial design. Many practical matters had to be considered before the design even became a blueprint. The walls had to be made longer than in Lin's original design; the many names to be included needed even more room than she had calculated. Then with the contractor who had been hired and the landscape architect, Henry Arnold, Lin tramped all over Constitution Gardens. They had to determine exactly where to place the memorial. It was important to have it in correct alignment with the imposing monuments on each side. Drainage problems and the water level of the site had to be considered also. Lin had said after she won the competition that she didn't know how to draft. She learned that summer, along with some other nitty-gritty details of construction. Although she was on hand for "consultation" regarding the work on the memorial, Lin also did whatever an apprentice architect was assigned to do. One of her jobs was designing water fountains for the upcoming New Orleans Exposition.

While Lin was learning, she did not forget that it was *her* work the architects were dealing with in their design development. She vetoed any attempt to make changes in the original design. Sometimes she felt that she was being treated as the greenest, most inexperienced of beginners. The attitude of the architects, she said, was like, "All right, you've done the design. It's real simple. We'll take it from there."[2] That, she decided was not going to happen. The design was hers, every aspect of it, so she did not hesitate to express her opinions. And the architects listened when they realized that this was a young woman who knew her own design. "I decided on everything, from the lettering to the sandblasting, to the alphabet style of the inscription," she said.[3]

Her experiences that year convinced Lin that architecture "is a very male-dominated profession," but

Maya Lin standing in Constitution Gardens. She and landscape architect Henry Arnold spent considerable time inspecting the site for the memorial.

she added, "I intend to succeed in it"[4] and to prove that "women can get things built."[5] She planned to continue study in graduate school and eventually to open her own office as a professional architect.

Once the controversy over the statue and the flag was settled—it was called Lin's "baptism by fire"[6]—the building of the memorial could begin. Bulldozers opened up the ground in March 1982, and the massive job got under way. The black marble for the walls came from India. Then it was shipped to Vermont, and stonecutters cut it into panels. These were polished to a high luster. From Vermont the panels went to Tennessee, where skilled workmen sandblasted the names on them.

Arranging the names beforehand had been a long, complicated process. The correct names of the servicemen had been researched along with their tours of duty. Then they were placed on the panels in the proper chronological order. That arrangement was an important part of Maya Lin's design. She had stated in the design's explanation that the names would begin and end in the center of the memorial, where the walls would meet. The name of the first person killed in the war would be inscribed at the top of one wall and the names of others would follow down to the end of that wall. On the other wall, the names would continue at the bottom and go upward until the last casualty's name was at the top, meeting the name of the first one. Thus, Maya said, "the war's beginning and end meet; the war is complete, coming full circle."[7]

The names of those soldiers missing in action were included with the names of those who had been killed. A small symbol next to each name indicates whether a person named is officially confirmed killed or is missing in action. The symbol would be changed if any missing in action servicemen are confirmed dead at some future time. Also, room was left on the panels of the walls to add more names when necessary—of those who have died since the end of the war as a result of war-caused wounds. Periodically, these names are added to the others on the Wall. The families of those servicemen make sure of that. Having a name inscribed on the Wall is honor and recognition, a reminder always to remember, never to forget. Maya Lin herself said, "The name is one of the most magical ways to bring back a person."[8]

The dedication of the Wall took place right on time, as scheduled in the VVMF's timetable—Veterans Day, 1982. That was only eight months after the actual construction was started. It was a remarkable feat. No other Washington monument had been built in such a short time.

The sheer enormity of the number of names on the Wall is so striking that at first it silences the people who see it. There is a hush similar to the feeling in a church or sanctuary. Then as people draw near to see the names,

President Ronald Reagan stood before the Vietnam Veterans Memorial on the day of its dedication, Veterans Day, 1982.

they touch and then they cry. The meaning of all those names is not lost. Further words are not needed. The almost universal effect of seeing the names on the Wall is as Maya Lin predicted. When she herself went there as a visitor for the first time, she said, "I searched out the name of a friend's father. I touched it and I cried. I was another visitor, and I was reacting to it as I had designed it."[9]

Maya Lin's intention in designing the memorial was realized, just as Jan Scruggs's was. With him, it was the determination to get 58,000 names, all of them, upon a wall that would stand forever. Maya Lin's purpose was more subjective. For her, the Wall would be honest about the reality of war just by listing the names of those who gave their lives: "Each name a special human being who never came home."[10] Although the memorial made no statement about the Vietnam War, the names alone "come across as a powerful antiwar statement."[11]

One writer, after the dedication of the Wall, said, "It is a book of the dead, listed in chronological order from the first one killed in 1959 to the last one in 1975."[12] Maya Lin's "Book of the Dead" can be read by everyone who visits the Wall.

In spite of her unhappiness about the controversy over the design and the drive for changes to it, Maya Lin had accomplished her purpose. The memorial would be there for all to see. Many people had been associated with the project of getting the memorial built, and many

The effect of the names on the Wall is not lost on visitors.

had opposed it—but it was Maya Lin's name that would be remembered. The memorial was hers, unique and different as it was, a break from memorials of the past. This one, stark and unadorned, with names instead of symbols, is the monument of today. It has influenced the style of many other memorials in cities and states across the country.

"You learn what you can from a piece and then move on."[1]
—*Maya Lin*

After the Wall

Maya Lin stayed in Washington, D.C., during the time the Vietnam Veterans Memorial was being constructed. She was still the "design consultant" and would be on hand until the design became reality. She admitted that she "couldn't wait to see her vision set in concrete."[2]

However, she did not enjoy living in Washington. She said she felt "suffocated" there, in that city of "power seekers."[3] She explained, "I feel I don't fit in and I never will."[4] Her favorite cities are New York, Boston, and San Francisco.

She was eager to get on with graduate studies, so in September 1982, she enrolled in Harvard University's Graduate School of Design. Every weekend she commuted from Cambridge, Massachusetts, to Washington, where she checked into a hotel room. She

Maya Lin outside her apartment in Cambridge, Massachusetts, in November 1982.

worked on her university assignments by night and on memorial problems by day. Sometimes a few flames of the controversy flared up again, but eventually died down. Disheartened as these episodes made her, Lin was still certain that when the people saw the memorial, they would accept it.

It was not long before the pressure of trying to do too much became unbearable. After staying up all night finishing a school paper, she decided, "I can't do this any more."[5] She quit her graduate work at Harvard, and soon after the dedication of the memorial, she left Washington. In a gesture of frustration and possibly to look older, she cropped her long hair. Lin was very self-conscious about her youthful appearance. She told Jonathan Coleman of *Time* that she was looking forward to becoming thirty.[6]

She moved to Boston, far enough away from Washington, and signed on with an architectural firm in that city. For the next year, she worked as an apprentice with professional architects. She helped in designing houses and, by herself, designed a stage set in Philadelphia. The various projects in which she was involved gave her practical experience and prepared her for further study.

By the fall of 1983, Lin was ready for a return to academic life. She decided to go back to Yale, her real alma mater. "I needed a place to start over," she told a reporter who interviewed her for *Newsweek*. "Yale was like going home."[7]

At Yale, Lin studied architecture under two renowned professors, Frank Gehry and Vincent Tully. Professor Tully was an architectural historian who had great admiration for Lin's Vietnam War Memorial. He called it a "moving," and "remarkable" monument.[8]

Two years after the memorial's dedication, on Veterans Day 1984, the subject of the Vietnam memorial was again prominent in the news. Frederick Hart's statue was unveiled and formally dedicated. It was, as specified, well away from the Wall. The complete memorial now included, besides the Wall and the statue, a large American flag atop a fifty-foot pole near the entrance plaza to the site. It was turned over to the National Park Service and thus became the responsibility of the United States government.

No member of the public who has visited the Vietnam Veteran's Memorial seems to question the presence of the statue. It is a larger than life bronze depiction of three young servicemen who wear the uniform and equipment of war. They stand looking tired and weary, as if gazing across a field, or as some visitors think, looking at the Wall commemorating the dead. A writer who described the statue thus said that the two parts of the memorial "were not separate—they seemed made for reconciliation."[9] Afterward, Maya Lin said, "In a funny sense, the compromise brings the memorial closer to the truth.

Frederick Hart's statue of three young servicemen was dedicated on
Veterans Day, 1984.

What is also memorialized is that people still cannot resolve that war, nor can they separate the issues, the politics, from it."[10]

Maya Lin was not in attendance at the 1984 dedication. Many people were not aware of the controversy over the statue and Lin's objection to it. Benjamin Forgey, a *Washington Post* reporter, wrote that Lin's name "unpardonably went unmentioned in the ceremony, but her presence was there for all to see: the great black wall, rising from and returning to grass-covered earth, exactly on axis with the Washington Monument and the Lincoln Memorial."[11]

Lin found time in between college semesters to be with her family. She traveled to Paris to see her brother who was studying there. Then in 1985 she went to China with her parents. While in the Orient, she worked for a while as an apprentice with a Japanese architect in Tokyo. Back home, Lin wrote about some of her architectural experiences in Asia. *The New Republic* published her article about outstanding new buildings in Hong Kong, skyscrapers that she said break from the more traditional style by being innovative, "futuristic...representing the 21st Century."[12] Some existing New York City skyscrapers she criticized as "inhuman, lifeless, monotonous," housing nothing more than "compartments."[13] Her opinions were clearly expressed and informative, revealing her own leaning toward the daringly new and modern style.

In 1986, Maya Lin was awarded a master's degree in architecture from Yale University. Just a year later, when she was only twenty-seven, Yale bestowed on her the honorary degree of doctor of fine arts. She was already one of the university's foremost alumni.

Around this time, she moved to New York City, where she established her permanent base in an old loft building in the Bowery, on the city's lower East Side. The building housed several other artists, most of them friends Lin had known at Yale. She shared a studio-apartment with a companion. Here, six flights up, Lin felt safe from curiosity seekers who would not expect a famous artist to be living in a nondescript building on the Bowery. Only a cat or two might wander in from the street to be adopted by the loft's tenants.

Guarding her privacy was important to Maya Lin. Being a celebrity was not something she sought. In fact, as she told Elizabeth Kastor of *The Washington Post,* she never wanted to be "troubled by fame."[14] Here in her chosen lifestyle, surrounded by other artists and friends, Lin could work quietly on her sculptures in a studio awash with blueprints, plans, and scale models, the walls covered with photos and sketches. She could dress casually, comfortably in her usual "thrift shop originals"[15] as she described her outfit of jeans, sneakers, and a rumpled jacket when Peter Tauber from the *New*

York Times Magazine interviewed her in her living quarters.

The sculptures that engrossed Lin when she was not designing architecture were, as Peter Tauber said, "slow to be made and quick to sell."[16] Composed of some of Lin's favorite materials, described as lead, broken glass, and mottled beeswax,[17] one piece might take a year to complete. Mostly hanging pieces, many of the sculptures were on display in the Sidney Janis Gallery and some in other galleries in New York City.

Maya Lin has never rejected sculpture for architecture. At graduate school, there were always suggestions from her professors that she should choose between the two. As she says, however, "I can't deny the other side of me."[18] She told Jill Kirschenbaum of *Ms.* that architecture is like writing a book, sculpture like composing a poem.[19] Sculpture is poetry in that it is one idea "stripped bare," whereas architecture is composed of many related ideas.

Lin received many requests for public appearances and lectures, most of which she turned down. One that she accepted in 1990 was at the Metropolitan Museum of Art in New York City. She told the overflow audience who came to hear her that "architects call me a sculptor and sculptors call me an architect." And she added humorously, "I don't think either one wants to claim me."[20]

In the meantime in Washington, another controversy about a statue was emerging. A group of women who had served with the American forces in the Vietnam War years decided that they deserved a statue too, on the site of the Vietnam Veterans Memorial. They became organized under the name Vietnam Women's Memorial Project (VWMP). Their aim was to have a statue honoring the women, all 250,000 who had been participants in some phase of the war effort. Ninety percent of that number were nurses; about 10,000 served in the armed forces; the rest were volunteers in the USO and Red Cross. The eight women who were killed in Vietnam—all nurses—have their names on the Wall.

The nurses of the United States Army Nurses Corps who served in Vietnam had seen firsthand all the horrors of the war. Their experiences there affected them deeply; many were emotionally scarred. Like the men who were in combat, they too suffered for years afterward from post-traumatic stress disorder, and many of them were helped to recover at the center set up in Menlo Park, New Jersey, by the Veterans Administration.

It took several years for the VWMP to achieve their goal of having a memorial statue for the Vietnam War's women veterans. Although the secretary of the interior approved the women's application to have their statue at Constitution Gardens, strong opposition arose about that location. Chief among the opponents was J. Carter Brown, the head of the Capitol's Fine Arts Commission. He had sided with Maya Lin when she objected to having the Three Servicemen Statue on the same site as the Wall. Commissioner Brown said the Vietnam memorial was "symbolically complete,"[21] and the placing of another statue near the Wall would encourage other organizations to follow suit. "It will never end,"[22] he predicted.

The influential Washington, D.C., newspaper, *The Washington Post*, kept abreast of the controversy. Journalist Benjamin Forgey wrote, "If we begin to single out veterans by gender, why not select them by ethnic groups...by specialties such as engineers, pilots, sergeants?"[23] An editorial in the *Post* agreed, declaring that although the plan to have a women's memorial was praiseworthy, the statue should be in another place. "Separate statues for special groups would detract from the whole," the *Post* argued, and continued, "Congress should leave this work of art alone."[24]

Many members of Congress endorsed the VWMF's desire to locate their statue on the site that the women wanted. But because of the opposition, Congress decided to hold hearings on the subject. Maya Lin returned to Washington in February 1988 to defend the position taken by the Fine Arts Commission. In the hearing, she maintained that the site of the Wall, being already complete, should not have any further additions imposed on it. She said that if this latest attempt to add another statue to the memorial was allowed, "It would be tampering with a national monument already approved."[25]

Congress delayed, and the arguments pro and con continued. The VWMP kept pressing for the site they wanted. They finally won their campaign when Congress voted to allow them to build a memorial statue on federal land. President Reagan signed the bill. A year later, in November 1989, President Bush signed legislation authorizing the placing of the statue within what is designated as "Area 1" of the Mall. That was the site of the Vietnam Veterans Memorial. In 1990, the Fine Arts Commission and the Memorial Planning Commission granted approval for the designated site, reluctantly. But a compromise of sorts was arranged. Although the statue was to be on the Vietnam Veterans Memorial grounds, it was to be as far from the Wall as possible—three hundred feet southeast of the Three Servicemen Statue.

The women veterans' memorial was completed by the sculptor Glenna Goodacre of New Mexico, and was dedicated on Veterans Day, 1993. It is called a "multi-figure sculpture in the round, portraying three Vietnam-era women, one of whom is caring for a wounded male soldier."[26] As described, "the statue will overlook the names etched on the wall."[27]

Laura Palmer in her article about the nurses of Vietnam said that, on Veterans Day, 1993, "a nation that never really noticed and hardly seemed to care...finally honored them with a memorial of their own."[28]

Except from the air, Maya Lin did not see the

The Vietnam Veterans Memorial as seen from the air. Maya Lin saw the memorial only this way for several years after she left Washington, D.C.

Vietnam Veterans Memorial for several years after she left Washington. As time went on however, in spite of the addition of the statues, she could feel satisfaction over her own accomplishment in creating the great centerpiece on the Mall. The statues can be considered footnotes to her awesome "Book of the Dead."

"The sound of the water is also very calming. Sound is important to me as an architect."[1]—*Maya Lin*

The Civil Rights Memorial

Lin had said, after she completed the Vietnam Veterans Memorial, that she would never design another war memorial.[2] The controversy over her design, with its political aspects, had discouraged her. So she retreated into her private life, did her own kind of work, sculptures, and accepted some private commissions, which she discovered she liked. "I'm interested in the psychology of the client,"[3] she said.

In the spring of 1988, Lin was at work in her loft studio when she received a call from a representative of the Southern Poverty Law Center of Montgomery, Alabama, known as the SPLC. The organization had been founded in 1971 to protect and advance the legal rights of poor people and minorities. The board of directors, headed by Morris Dees, the founder, had decided that they wanted a civil rights memorial on the plaza adjacent to their headquarters in Montgomery. One of the SPLC trustees said they should commission a top-notch architect for the job. The name of Maya Lin came immediately to mind. Her address in New York was not known then to the SPLC, and as Morris Dees recalled, "we phoned every Lin in the New York phone book"[4] before Maya Lin was reached.

Asked to design a civil rights memorial, Lin did not immediately agree. She did say she would read the material the SPLC wished to send her and would consider the matter. She took some time to do this, and then she decided to accept the commission. The historical significance of the civil rights movement impressed her. She was surprised that there was no such memorial already in existence. She was also concerned that she herself knew so little about the movement, never having studied it in school. Of course she was a very young child during the 1960s when the marches and the landmark decisions had occurred. She was only eight when Martin Luther King, Jr., was assassinated. Lin said that although there were specific monuments to certain people connected with the civil rights movement, "No memorial existed that encompassed the movement itself and caught what the whole era was about. It had been very much a people's movement—many people gave their lives for it, and that had been largely forgotten."[5]

After agreeing to design the memorial, Lin had to see

the site. On the plane going to Montgomery, she reread some of the words of Dr. King. She came across—again—what he said in several of his speeches. "We will not be satisfied until justice rolls down like waters, and righteousness like a mighty stream."[6] The words are taken from the book of Amos in the Old Testament. "Suddenly," Lin said, "something clicked," and the form took shape. "The minute I hit that quote I knew that the whole piece had to be about water."[7] The longer she considered it, the more certain she was. "I wanted to work with water, and I wanted to use the words [of Dr. King] because that's the clearest way to remember history."[8]

She kept thinking about the form of the memorial as she continued her journey. It also occurred to her that in the warm climate of Alabama, the cooling effect of flowing water would be appropriate. When she met the members of the SPLC at lunch in Montgomery, she quickly sketched what she had in mind on a paper napkin. After lunch, at the site where the memorial would stand, Lin saw the possibilities—and the need for rearranging some existing features there. It was agreed that she would start on the design as soon as she returned to New York.

Montgomery was a meaningful city for establishing a civil rights memorial. Only a few blocks away from the site was the Dexter Avenue Baptist Church were Dr. Martin Luther King, Jr., had preached. Montgomery was also the place where in 1965 the famous march from Selma ended. Led by Dr. King, that march was a demonstration on behalf of civil and voting rights for black people. Before that, in 1955, Montgomery was in the headlines as the place where Rosa Parks, riding on a city bus, refused to give up her seat to a white person and was arrested. The result was a boycott of the public buses in Montgomery by black people, also led by Dr. King. The boycott went on for over a year, during which no black persons in Montgomery rode the city buses. Finally, the U.S. Supreme Court ruled in favor of the protesters and outlawed bus segregation.

Morris Dees and his organization fought the Klu Klux Klan in court many times over the years. Lawsuits were won by the SPLC against the Klan for its hate crimes and attacks on civil rights leaders and buildings. The SPLC sponsors various projects to fight racial violence, among them Klanwatch, which takes legal action against offenders, and Teaching Tolerance, which develops educational materials and distributes them across America. To show her commitment to the cause, Maya Lin became a member of the advisory board of the SPLC's Teaching Tolerance project.

The Southern Poverty Law Center's plan in 1988 was to memorialize those individuals who had been killed in the course of marches and demonstrations for civil rights. On the memorial, their names and the names of landmark events in the civil rights struggle would be etched on stone. The research of records was done by Sara Bullard, one of the directors of the SPLC and the editor of the Center's book about the civil rights movement, *Free at Last.* Fifty-three significant entries would be inscribed on the memorial. When Lin saw that list, she said she realized that creating a time line was the way to highlight those names and events. They would be listed in chronological order from the first—"17 May 1954, the Supreme Court ruling outlawing school segregation" to the last, "4 April 1968, Martin Luther King, Jr. assassinated." There would be room at both ends for additions if related names and events were discovered.

Back in her studio, Lin started work on the project. The memorial she had decided to design would be in two parts and was scheduled to be dedicated in the fall of 1989. There would be a huge granite disk, or table, twelve feet in diameter, inscribed with the fifty-three names and events. The table, with the names arranged chronologically in a circle around the perimeter, would look something like a sundial. Behind the large disk there would be a black granite wall, nine feet high, which would be inscribed with the words of Dr. King that had inspired Lin's design.

In the completed, functioning memorial, water flows down the wall in a gentle cascade over those words. The table below the wall was designed to be less than three feet from the ground, made low so that children could reach it. The table, narrower at the bottom, from a

The Civil Rights Memorial in Montgomery, Alabama, designed by Maya Lin.

distance appears to be floating in air. Water rising from the center of the table spreads over it, covering the time line of names and events, which are still clearly seen through the veil of water. Visitors would be expected to touch the names as they walk around the table.

In the fall of 1988, not long after Lin had completed the civil rights memorial design, fire broke out in the building where she lived and worked. Fortunately, she had, some time before, mailed the model she'd made to the SPLC in Montgomery. But before the fire was controlled, much of the work of the artists who resided in the loft building was destroyed. Most of Maya Lin's sculptures were in the Sidney Janis Gallery, so her loss was minimal. But as she explained to Elizabeth Kastor who interviewed her shortly after the fire,[9] she, like many other artists, often destroyed a finished sculpture or other work if for some reason, she was not satisfied with it. She would start over. So would her friends. No one was injured in the fire, and the building was quickly repaired.

The Civil Rights Memorial was dedicated on time, although it had been complicated and difficult to construct. Ken Upchurch, who supervised the construction, said, when he first viewed the design, it was a "contractor's nightmare."[10] The day before the memorial was to be unveiled, the workers as well as the anxious SPLC people wondered if the water was going to work as well as it was supposed to. Last-minute adjustments took the workmen well into the night. Then when the memorial was finally, hopefully, ready, all those present held their breath as the water was turned on. A cheer went up when the water began its slow movement down the wall and across the table. Ken Upchurch said, "It worked perfectly."[11] A native of Montgomery, Upchurch said he learned more about the civil rights movement from constructing the memorial than he ever had before.

Besides being visited by families, friends, and relatives of those whose names are there, the memorial attracts people from all over. Tourists come or stop off in Montgomery to see it. As Maya Lin had hoped, the memorial has become an educational experience. Schoolchildren come, and learn. Maya Lin, who aimed always for simplicity, said of the Civil Rights Memorial, "A child can understand it. You don't need to read an art history book to understand it."[12] One little girl said, "It makes you want to touch the names with your fingers, and talk about what happened."[13] Like touching the names on the Vietnam Wall, this memorial, too, evokes tears from the many people who visit it.

Maya Lin was impressed, as she said, with the powerful effect that "words joined with water would generate."[14] She was "surprised and moved when people started to cry...tears were becoming part of the memorial, as William Zinsser wrote in *Smithsonian*."[15]

Lin received unqualified praise for her part in this

memorial. Unlike the Vietnam Veterans Memorial, this one was happily free from controversy over its merits. One writer commented, "She has once again created an architectural masterpiece."[16] Lin herself said, "I've been incredibly fortunate to have been given the opportunity to work on not just one but both memorials."[17]

Morris Dees said about the memorial she created for the Southern Poverty Law Center, "You can't put something better located than Montgomery, where everything happened, and you can't get anyone better than Maya Lin to do it."[18]

"I work with the landscape, and I hope that the object and the land are equal partners."[1]*—Maya Lin*

Landscape Solutions

Late in 1989, Maya Lin accepted the first of two important outdoor design commissions. She had always had a strong interest in landscape architecture. Also, successful as the Vietnam Veterans Memorial and the Civil Rights Memorial were, she did not want to be labeled forever as a war memorial designer—and nothing else. There was a great deal she wanted to do and a whole career lay ahead of her.

Lin's first landscape design was for a Peace Chapel at Juniata College in Huntingdon, Pennsylvania. Elizabeth Evans Baker and John Baker, the donors of the chapel, were friends of Lin's parents. Mr. Baker had been the president of Ohio University from 1945 to 1961, during the time that Julia and Henry Lin had joined the faculty there. The two families became good friends.

After Mr. Baker retired from Ohio University, he and his wife devoted themselves to the cause of world peace. They established the department of peace studies at Juniata, where Mr. Baker, a graduate of the college in 1917, served on the board of trustees.

Maya Lin said that she would never have envisioned doing this landscape project if Mrs. Baker had not asked her to design an open-air chapel for Juniata College. "It was the relationship of the two families"[2] and also, Lin said, the college's concern for world peace that brought her to Juniata.

The Peace Chapel was to be an open-air place where people could go for contemplation and for nondenominational church services. The location, about a mile from the college, was a protected bird sanctuary, owned and preserved by Juniata. Maya Lin said that Mrs. Baker's ideas for an open-air chapel at this place "interested me from the start."[3] When she went to Huntingdon to inspect the site of the proposed chapel, she saw that she could not improve upon the location, a beautiful meadow set into the surrounding hills overlooking the college. It was a perfect place for the Peace Chapel.

The choice of Maya Lin was praised by Juniata's community—faculty and alumni alike. It was noted in the October 1989 alumni bulletin that the young artist's talent in relating a structure to its site was outstanding. The Vietnam Veterans Memorial was known as "a great work of landscape architecture," and one of the nation's "most respected works of public art."[4]

Lin designed the Peace Chapel in two parts. The first consisted of a large circle of rough-hewn stones, huge blocks on which people would sit. The circle, forty feet in diameter, as Lin explained at the dedication ceremony, is a form that denotes symmetry and equality. Everyone sitting around it would be equal, with no "centerpiece"[5] or other arrangement that would rank or separate the group. "A very simple design," she said.[6]

The second part of the chapel reflects the first. It is a smaller circle, only five feet in diameter, set on a ridge, several feet above the first ring. Overlooking the larger circle, it is designed for private or individual reflection. Rough stones similar to the lower ones form the small circle. "One person can quietly sit there and contemplate, think...the two-part design frames the two ways in which we think, in which we gather," Lin explained.[7]

Juniata College's Peace Chapel carries out Maya Lin's basic ideas about structures and land being related. Buildings that seem to grow from the earth, framed by the landscape, become part of it. The rough-hewn stones of the Peace Chapel, deliberately chosen to avoid a "manicured" look, will in time, Lin said, be covered with moss and surrounded by grass.[8] There will be "quietly implied order," in harmony with nature. Maya

The open-air Peace Chapel designed by Maya Lin for Juniata
College, Huntingdon, Pennsylvania.

Lin's feeling for simplicity is notable, never more so than in this open-air chapel.

As writer Peter Tauber commented, "Sometimes the most important lesson at a site is understanding what not to do." Basically, he said, Maya Lin "simply cleared a sitting space for open-air meditation."[9]

From the Peace Chapel, Lin went on to another landscape design in Charlotte, North Carolina, in 1990. Called "an environmental art work,"[10] the outdoor project was created for the Charlotte Coliseum, a sports stadium. It was sponsored by the city's planning commission in an unusual—and successful—effort to beautify the surroundings of a sports complex.

Lin decided that she would use giant topiary bushes to carry out her theme. These would be planted on the long traffic approach to the coliseum. (Topiary landscaping is trimming or shaping trees or shrubbery into ornamental shapes. It is an admired feature of many famous gardens, especially in the southern states.) Lin brought in landscape architect Henry Arnold to work with her. It was he who had designed Constitution Gardens in Washington, D.C., the site of the Vietnam Veterans Memorial. He had also advised Lin about the landscape problems connected with that site.

For this project in Charlotte, Lin wanted holly bushes to be trimmed into giant balls to carry out the sports theme of her design. They would, once planted, grow on the sloping plane of ground that slanted down

Maya Lin's topiary design for the Charlotte, North Carolina Coliseum. The people of Charlotte call it "Topo."

to the coliseum. But finding holly bushes as large as Lin needed was not easy. A landscape consultant in Charlotte searched the city for them. Finally, he found ten huge holly bushes on the circular drive of an old house. The owner agreed to sell them. Then they were excavated and planted on the site of the coliseum project.

Problems as huge as the holly bushes had to be solved before the specimens were in place. Drainage, grading, retaining walls—all were tackled, with the help of many workmen and heavy machinery. Lin found herself, a lone female, telling a crew of burly laborers what she wanted them to do.[11] That did not daunt her. She had said more than once that women, too, can learn to build things.[12] Henry Arnold noted that Maya Lin appeared to enjoy the lighthearted aspect of this design and the effect it would have on people.

A writer who observed the landscape design taking shape described it as "a giant, droll topiary park" with holly bushes appearing "to be rolling downhill one after another."[13] Lin called it "surreal, absolutely fun—a stage set the public can be part of."[14]

The whimsy of the coliseum's landscape appearance is appreciated by the people in Charlotte. They call it "Topo."

"I used to be terrified that at 21, I might already have outdone myself. Now I'm too busy to think about it." [1]

—*Maya Lin*

Architect and Artist

By 1990, awards and design commissions were coming to Maya Lin one after the other. A grant from the National Endowment for the Arts enabled her to do some of the things she enjoyed most. She worked on many sculpture pieces. Some of them were put on display at galleries, others were privately commissioned.

In 1990, Lin was asked by Yale University's president, Benno Schmidt, to design a memorial to honor the presence of women in the university. The memorial would actually celebrate the years of women students' presence at Yale. It was especially appropriate for one of Yale's most distinguished alumnae to create such a memorial. Yale had been home to Maya Lin as an undergraduate and graduate student for seven years in all.

The memorial, when completed, was to be installed

on Cross Campus, Yale's main quadrangle. Across from the central college library, it is where students gather to "hang out and just be part of the campus,"[2] as Lin said. The memorial itself is a low, polished green granite oval, set on a stone base, not much over three feet high. As in the Civil Rights Memorial, water flows gently over the oval "table." Under the water, the dates of important events and their meanings in Yale's history are inscribed. Starting in 1701, Yale's beginning, the dates are listed in order—up to 1969, when women were admitted. This signified, as Maya said,[3] that the memorial for women is more about the future than commemorating the past. Fifteen dates of future events concerning women at Yale will be added. Up to the placing of this memorial, all of the statues and plaques located around the campus have been for men. The "Women's Table" is a first.

The Gleitsman Foundation in Malibu, California, commissioned Maya Lin to design a sculpture for their philanthropic organization. The foundation each year honors one person who has helped bring about social change.[4] One of the first recipients honored for courage in confronting problems and challenging dangerous conditions was Lois Gibbs, who fought to clean up Love Canal, the area near Niagara Falls, New York, that was contaminated by toxic waste. Each recipient of the award is given $100,000 and the specially commissioned and commemorative sculpture designed by Maya Lin. The sculpture resembles in size and appearance a small,

Maya Lin working at her desk in her New York City studio.

tabletop television model, but instead of a screen, it encloses a glass centerpiece. In Maya Lin's design description, she says that the sculpture is meant to honor "those exceptional people who have seen our world with a clearer perception, as if it were magnified, and this sculpture "embodies that clarity of vision these people have."[5]

The Gleitsman Foundation continues to honor and award those individuals who take on and try to solve the problems of social injustice.

The Metropolitan Transit Authority of New York City commissioned Maya Lin to do an art work for the new Penn Station concourse. She designed a futuristic-style clock, fourteen feet wide, to be set into a recess in the vaulted ceiling of the station. Unveiled in August 1994, "Eclipsed Time" as Maya Lin calls her work, was described by writers who interviewed her as resembling a "glowing flying saucer,"[6] and as a "gorgeous overhead solar system of a clock."[7] It will certainly be an object of great attention when the Penn Station Improvement project is completed and people pass through the terminal where the new 34th Street entrance and the 7th Avenue subway meet.

Another indoor project Lin designed was opened to the public in 1993. The sponsors of the Museum of African Art in New York City selected her to design the interior of the two lower floors of their remodeled building in lower Manhattan.

As *The New York Times* art critic, Herbert Muschamp said, she designed a "flowing sequence of galleries."[8] She used different colors, materials, and lighting as well as curving walls to help the flow from one area to another. The museum features all aspects of African life and culture, from ritual emblems and altars to sculptures and handicrafts. This type of project was one that Maya Lin welcomed. A few years earlier, she had said, "I can see doing an art museum or a school."[9]

A recent project for Lin has been designing a group of architectural and sculptural works for the Wexner Center for the Arts at Ohio State University in Columbus, Ohio. The aim of the center is to foster the arts of our time and in so doing provide a "time and an environment in which artists can work."[10] Residency awards are given to artists in various fields; this allows them to live and work at the university for a certain period of time in order to create or complete their projects. Maya Lin's residency resulted in bringing together the two forms of art for which she is known—architecture and sculpture. Some of her "private," small-scale works will be in the indoor gallery, while her "public" work, architecture, can be seen in the space surrounding the Art Center's main building. Called "Groundswell," this three-level garden of sea-green crushed glass evoked one unpleasant response. Carol Vogel of *The New York Times* who interviewed Maya Lin, said, "Somebody who didn't like the work poured red pigment over a large portion of it."[11] Tons of the glass had to be replaced, and although Lin said she took it personally, and felt pain, then anger, she added, "I've learned to expect criticism when you do anything public."[12]

Lin has gone from east to west, designing unique homes. One in Williamstown, Massachusetts, has been described as a "low-slung Japanese-inspired, courtyard house," and one in Santa Monica, California, as "a vertical, steel and glass house."[13] She also designed an addition to her own family home in Athens, Ohio, where her mother still lives. (Professor Henry Lin died in 1989.)

There will be many more forms of art and architecture designed by Maya Lin. She was once afraid that the Vietnam Veterans Memorial would define her work ever after, that she would be remembered for that only. Her accomplishments since then have proved that she is, and will continue to be, an artist as well as an architect.

Inevitably, however, the Vietnam Veterans Memorial will be part of her life, a landmark in her career. On every Veterans Day, Americans pause to remember and honor the men and women who served—and the many who died for their country. That memorial in Washington, D.C., is now where our national leaders observe the rites of remembrance. On Veterans Day, 1992, on the tenth anniversary of the Wall, Maya Lin sat

Maya Lin with Vice President-elect Al Gore at the tenth anniversary commemoration of the Vietnam Veterans Memorial, in 1992.

among the notables. She was no longer the youthful student who had impulsively cropped her long hair in order to look older. She was a celebrity in her own right now, sitting beside Vice President-elect Gore at the Veterans Day ceremonies. In a way, that marked her own reconciliation to the furor, now past, over the design of the Vietnam Veterans Memorial. When she had accepted the Presidential Design Award in 1988, she also received the tribute that accompanied it. "This one superb design has changed the way war memorials are perceived."[14]

Chronology

1959—On October 5, 1959, Maya Ying Lin was born to Henry Huan Lin and Julia Chang Lin.

1965—Attended public schools in Athens, Ohio.
-1977

1977—Graduated from Athens High School.

1977—Attended Yale University.
-1981

1981—Announced as the winner of the Vietnam Veterans Memorial design competition.

1981—Graduated from Yale with a bachelor of arts degree.

1981—Worked as a design consultant with an
-1982 architectural firm in Washington, D.C.

1982—Left Washington for Harvard University, where she enrolled in the Graduate School of Design.

1983—Returned to Yale University as a graduate student in architecture.

1983—Worked on various architectural projects.
-1985

1986—Received master's degree in architecture from Yale.

1987—Was awarded honorary doctor of fine arts degree from Yale.

1988—Received Presidential Design Award for the Vietnam Veterans Memorial.

1988—Began work on the Civil Rights Memorial for the Southern Poverty Law Center in Montgomery, Alabama.

1989—Attended dedication of the Civil Rights Memorial.

1989—Designed a topiary landscape project for the Charlotte, North Carolina, Coliseum.

1989—Designed the outdoor Peace Chapel for Juniata College in Huntingdon, Pennsylvania.

1990—Was awarded a grant from the National Endowment for the Arts.

1991—Designed the "Women's Table" at Yale University as a memorial honoring women students at Yale.

1992—Attended the tenth anniversary celebration of the Vietnam Veterans Memorial.

1993—Designed the interior of the lower two floors of Museum of African Art in New York City.

1993—Received an artist residency award from the Wexner Center for the Arts at Ohio State University in Columbus, Ohio.

1994—Designed "Eclipsed Time," a ceiling clock for Penn Station concourse in New York City.

Chapter Notes

Chapter 1

1. Jill Kirschenbaum, "The Symmetry of Maya Lin," *Ms.*, September/October 1990, p. 20.

2. United Press International, "Student Wins War Memorial Contest," *The New York Times*, May 7, 1981, p. 20.

3. Christopher Buckley, "The Wall," *Esquire*, September 1985, p. 66.

4. Jan C. Scruggs and Joel L. Swerdlow, *To Heal a Nation: The Vietnam Veterans Memorial* (New York: Harper and Row, 1985), p. 64.

5. Wolf Von Eckhardt, "The Making of a Memorial," *The Washington Post*, April 26, 1980, p. C7.

6. Joel L. Swerdlow, "To Heal a Nation," adapted from the book by Jan C. Scruggs and Joel L. Swerdlow, *National Geographic*, May 1985, p. 566.

7. United Press International, p. 20.

8. B. Drummond Ayres, Jr., "A Yale Senior, A Vietnam Memorial and a Few Ironies," *The New York Times*, June 29, 1981, p. B5.

9. Benjamin Forgey, "The Statue and the Wall," *The Washington Post*, November 10, 1984, p. D1.

10. Alan Borg, *War Memorials from Antiquity to the Present* (London: Cooper, 1991), p. 74.

11. Henry Allen, "Epitaph for Vietnam," *The Washington Post*, May 7, 1981, p. F1.

Chapter 2

1. Jonathan Coleman, "First She Looks Inward," *Time*, November 26, 1989, p. 90.

2. Phil McCombs, "Maya Lin and the Great Call of China," *The Washington Post*, January 3, 1982, p. F9.

3. Ibid.

4. Peter Tauber, "Monument Maker," *The New York Times Magazine*, February 24, 1991, p. 55.

5. McCombs, p. F9.

6. B. Drummond Ayres, Jr., "A Yale Senior, a Vietnam Memorial and a Few Ironies," *The New York Times*, June 29, 1981, p. B5.

7. McCombs, p. F9.

8. Ibid.

9. Ibid.

10. Tauber, p. 5.

11. Carol Kramer, "The Wall: Monument to a Nation's Sacrifice," *McCall's*, June 1988, pp. 42–45.

12. McCombs, p. F10.

13. Coleman, p. 92.

14. McCombs, p. F9.

15. Coleman, p. 92.

16 Brent Ashabranner, *Always to Remember: The Story of the Vietnam Veterans Memorial* (New York: Putnam, 1988), p. 39.

17. Maya Lin, letter to author (January 1993).

Chapter 3

1. Peter Tauber, "Monument Maker," *The New York Times Magazine*, February 24, 1991, p. 55.

2. Phil McCombs, "Maya Lin and the Great Call of China," *The Washington Post*, January 3, 1982, p. F9.

3. Ibid.

4. B. Drummond Ayres, Jr., "A Yale Senior, a Vietnam Memorial and a Few Ironies," *The New York Times*, June 29, 1981, p. B5.

5. McCombs, p. F9.

6. Ibid., p. F1.

7. Ayres, p. B5.

8. McCombs, p. F9.

9. Jonathan Coleman, "First She Looks Inward," *Time*, November 26, 1989, p. 92.

10. Lilly Wei, "Maya Lin Interview," *Art in America*, September 1991, p. 128.

Chapter 4

1. B. Drummond Ayres, Jr., "A Yale Senior, a Vietnam Memorial and a Few Ironies," *The New York Times*, June 29, 1981, p. B5.

2. Jan C. Scruggs and Joel L. Swerdlow, *To Heal a Nation: The Vietnam Veterans Memorial* (New York: Harper and Row, 1985), pp. 7–8.

3. Arthur C. Danto, "The Vietnam Veterans Memorial," *The Nation*, August 31, 1985, p. 154.

4. Wolf Von Eckhardt, "The Making of a Memorial," *The Washington Post*, April 26, 1980, p. C7.

5. Scruggs and Swerdlow, p. 58.

6. Ibid.

7. Ayres, p. B5.

8. Ibid.

9. Edward Clinton Ezell, *Reflections on the Wall: The Vietnam Memorial* (Harrisburg, Penn.: Stackpole Books, 1987), p. 16.

10. Joel L. Swerdlow, "To Heal a Nation," adapted from the book by Jan C. Scruggs and Joel L. Swerdlow, *National Geographic*, May 1985, p. 557.

11. Phil McCombs, "Maya Lin and the Great Call of China," *The Washington Post*, January 3, 1982, p. F4.

12. Wolf Von Eckhardt, "Of Heart and Mind," *The Washington Post*, May 16, 1981, p. B1.

13. "Vietnam Memorial Architect Presents Keynote Address," *Bulletin Juniata College Alumni*, November 1989, p. 14.

14. Maya Lin, "Interview," *National Geographic*, May 1985, p. 557.

15. Maya Lin, "Letter to the Editor," *The New York Times*, July 14, 1981, p. 24.

16. Henry Allen, "Epitaph for Vietnam," *The Washington Post*, May 7, 1981, p. F1.

17. Maya Lin, "Interview," *National Geographic*, May 1985, p. 557.

18. Scruggs and Swerdlow, pp. 66–67.

19. Ibid.

20. Maya Lin, letter to author (January 1993).

Chapter 5

1. Elizabeth Kastor, "Maya Lin's Unwavering Vision," *The Washington Post*, February 13, 1989, p. B6.

2. Jan C. Scruggs and Joel L. Swerdlow, *To Heal a Nation: The Vietnam Veterans Memorial* (New York: Harper and Row, 1985), p. 79.

3. Elizabeth Hess, "A Tale of Two Memorials," *Art in America*, April 1983, p. 122.

4. Jonathan Coleman, "First She Looks Inward," *Time*, November 1989, p. 90.

5. Ibid.

6. Michael J. Weiss, "The Vietnam War Dead Raises Hope—and Anger," *People Weekly*, March 8, 1982, p. 39.

7. Coleman, p. 90.

8. Phil McCombs, "Maya Lin and the Great Call of China," *The Washington Post*, January 3, 1982, p. F1.

9. Ibid.

10. Scruggs and Swerdlow, p. 56.

11. Joel L. Swerdlow, "To Heal a Nation," adapted from the book by Jan C. Scruggs and Joel L. Swerdlow, *National Geographic*, May 1985, p. 557.

12. Hess, pp. 125–126.

13. Wolf Von Eckhardt, "Storm over a Vietnam Memorial," *Time*, November 9, 1981, p. 103.

14. Weiss, p. 83.

15. Benjamin Forgey, "The Statue and the Wall," *The Washington Post*, November 10, 1984, p. D8.

16. Scruggs and Swerdlow, p. 56.

17. Ibid.

18. B. Drummond Ayres, Jr., "A Yale Senior, a Vietnam Memorial and a Few Ironies," *The New York Times*, June 29, 1981, p. B5.

19. Scruggs and Swerdlow, p. 64.

20. Ibid.

21. Wolf Von Eckhardt, "Of Heart and Mind," *The Washington Post*, May 16, 1981, p. B4.

22. Ibid.

23. Washington Diarist, "Downcast Eyes," *The New Republic*, November 28, 1982, p. 42.

24. Hess, p. 122.

25. Isabel Wilkerson, "Art War Erupts over Vietnam Veterans Memorial," *The Washington Post*, July 8, 1982, p. D3.

26. Scruggs and Swerdlow, p. 101.

27. Ibid., p. 80.

Chapter 6

1. Michael J. Weiss, "The Vietnam War Dead Raises Hope—and Anger" *People Weekly*, March 8, 1982, p. 38.

2. Elizabeth Kastor, "Maya Lin's Unwavering Vision," *The Washington Post,* February 3, 1989, p. B6.

3. Weiss, p. 38.

4. Brent Ashabranner, *Always to Remember: The Story of the Vietnam Veterans Memorial* (New York: Putnam, 1988), p. 92.

5. Lilly Wei, "Maya Lin Interview," *Art in America,* September 1991, pp. 127–128.

6. Peter Tauber, "Monument Maker," *The New York Times Magazine,* February 24, 1991, p. 53.

7. Ashabranner, p. 55.

8. "Model of Civil Rights Memorial Unveiled," *The New York Times,* July 30, 1988, p. 7.

9. Joel L. Swerdlow, "To Heal a Nation," adapted from the book by Jan C. Scruggs and Joel L. Swerdlow, *National Geographic,* May 1985, p. 557.

10. Ibid., p. 572.

11. Elizabeth Hess, "A Tale of Two Memorials," *Art in America,* April 1983, p. 126.

12. Arthur C. Danto, "The Vietnam Veterans Memorial," *The Nation,* August 31, 1985, p. 154.

Chapter 7

1. Elizabeth Kastor, "Maya Lin's Unwavering Vision," *The Washington Post,* February 13, 1989, p. B6.

2. Michael J. Weiss, "The Vietnam War Dead Raises Hope—and Anger," *People Weekly,* March 8, 1982, p. 39.

3. Phil McCombs, "Maya Lin and the Great Call of China," *The Washington Post,* January 3, 1982, p. F11.

4. Ibid.

5. Maggie Malone, "Up Against the Wall," *Newsweek,* January 20, 1986, p. 6.

6. Jonathan Coleman, "First She Looks Inward," *Time*, November 1989, p. 96.

7. Malone, p. 6.

8. McCombs, p. F12.

9. Benjamin Forgey, "The Statue and the Wall," *The Washington Post*, November 10, 1984, p. D8.

10. James M. Mayo, *War Memorials as Political Landscape* (New York: Praeger, 1988), p. 205.

11. Forgey, p. D8.

12. Maya Lin, "Beauty and the Bank," *The New Republic*, December 23, 1985, pp. 25–29.

13. Ibid.

14. Kastor, p. B6.

15. Peter Tauber, "Monument Maker," *The New York Times Magazine*, February 24, 1991, p. 50.

16. Ibid.

17. Beeswax is a plastic, readily-molded substance, which comes from the wax secreted by bees for making the honeycomb.

18. Kastor, p. B6.

19. Jill Kirschenbaum, "The Symmetry of Maya Lin," *Ms.*, September/October 1990, pp. 20–21.

20. Tauber, p. 50.

21. Benjamin Forgey, "Commission Vetoes Vietnam Women's Statue," *The Washington Post*, October 23, 1987, p. B1.

22. Ibid.

23. Benjamin Forgey, "Women and the Wall," *The Washington Post*, October 22, 1987, p. E1.

24. Editorial, *The Washington Post*, November 11, 1987, p. A22.

25. Karen Swisher, "Maya Lin's Memorial Defense," *The Washington Post*, February 24, 1988, p. C1.

26. "A Legacy of Healing and Hope," *Vietnam Women's Memorial Project Inc.* (Washington, D.C., February/March 1993).

27. Ibid.

28. Laura Palmer, "How to Bandage a War," *The New York Times Magazine*, November 7, 1993, p. 8.

Chapter 8

1. William Zinsser, "I Realized Her Tears Were Becoming Part of the Memorial," *Smithsonian*, September 1991, p. 38.

2. Jonathan Coleman, "First She Looks Inward," *Time*, November 26, 1989, p. 92.

3. Charles Gandee, "Gandee at Large," *House and Garden*, March 1990, p. 214.

4. Peter Tauber, "Monument Maker," *The New York Times Magazine*, February 24, 1991, p. 55.

5. Zinsser, p. 36.

6. Southern Poverty Law Center, *Free at Last: A History of the Civil Rights Movement and Those Who Died in the Struggle* (Montgomery, Alabama: Southern Poverty Law Center, 1989), p. 104.

7. Jill Kirschenbaum, "The Symmetry of Maya Lin," *Ms.*, September/October 1990, p. 22.

8. Zinsser, p. 36.

9. Elizabeth Kastor, "Maya Lin's Unwavering Vision," *The Washington Post*, February 12, 1989, p. B6.

10. Coleman, p. 94.

11. Zinsser, p. 39.

12. Kastor, p. B6.

13. Kate Christensen, "A Civilized Memorial," *Seventeen*, June 1990, p. 40.

14. Zinsser, p. 35.

15. Ibid.

16. David Grogan, "Maya Lin Lets Healing Waters Flow over Her Civil Rights Memorial," *People Weekly*, November 20, 1989, p. 79.

17. Gandee, p. 214.

18. Kastor, p. B6.

Chapter 9

1. Elizabeth Hess, "A Tale of Two Memorials," *Art in America*, April 1983, p. 123.

2. "Vietnam Memorial Architect Presents Keynote Address," *Bulletin Juniata College Alumni*, November 1989, p. 14.

3. Ibid.

4. Ibid.

5. Maya Lin, "Reflections on Art Within Society," *Juniata College Convocation Address*, October 14, 1989, p. 2.

6. Maya Lin, "Remarks at Peace Chapel Dedication," *Juniata College*, October 14, 1989, p. 1.

7. Ibid.

8. Ibid.

9. Peter Tauber, "Monument Maker," *The New York Times Magazine*, February 24, 1991, p. 55.

10. Ibid., p. 52.

11. Ibid.

12. Lilly Wei, "Maya Lin Interview," *Art in America*, September 1991, p. 128.

13. Tauber, p. 52.

14. Ibid.

Chapter 10

1. Maggie Malone, "Up Against the Wall," *Newsweek*, January 20, 1986, p. 6.

2. Diana West, "A Monument of One's Own," *The American Spectator*, May 1992, p. 58.

3. Ibid.

4. "For People Who Make a Difference," *Statement of Purpose* (Malibu, Calif., The Gleitsman Foundation, 1993).

5. Ibid.

6. Peter Plagens and Yahlin Chang, "Maya Lin's Time for Light," *Newsweek*, August 8, 1994, p. 52.

7. The Talk of the Town, "Maya Lin's Moment," *The New Yorker*, July 11, 1994.

8. Herbert Muschamp, "Crossing Cultural Boundaries," *The New York Times*, February 12, 1993, p. C1.

9. Carol Kramer, "The Wall," *McCall's*, June 1988, p. 45.

10. Wexner Center for the Arts, "Maya Lin Artist Residency Project Update," *Ohio State University Wexner Center for the Arts*, May 21, 1993.

11. Carol Vogel, "Maya Lin's World Of Architecture, Or is It Art?" *The New York Times*, May 9, 1994, p. C11.

12. Ibid.

13. Charles Gandee, "People Are Talking About Maya Lin," *Vogue*, February 1993, p. 61.

14. Jill Kirschenbaum, "The Symmetry of Maya Lin," *Ms.*, September/October 1990, p. 20.

Further Reading

Ashabranner, Brent. *Always to Remember: The Story of the Vietnam Veterans Memorial.* New York: Putnam, 1988.

Borg, Alan. *War Memorials from Antiquity to the Present.* London: Cooper, 1991.

Ezell, Edward Clinton. *Reflections on the Wall: The Vietnam Memorial.* Harrisburg, Penn.: Stackpole Books, 1987.

Katakis, Michael. *The Vietnam Veterans Memorial.* New York: Crown, 1988.

Mayo, James M. *War Memorials as Political Landscape.* New York: Praeger, 1988.

Morse, George L. *Fallen Soldiers: Reshaping the Memory of the World Wars.* New York: Oxford University Press, 1990.

Scruggs, Jan C., and Joel L. Swerdlow, *To Heal a Nation: The Vietnam Veterans Memorial.* New York: Harper and Row, 1985.

Southern Poverty Law Center. *Free at Last: A History of the Civil Rights Movement and Those Who Died in the Struggle.* Montgomery, Ala.: Southern Poverty Law Center, 1989.

Spence, Jonathan D. *The Gate of Heavenly Peace.* New York: Viking Press, 1981.

Strait, Jerry L, and Sandra S. Strait, *Vietnam War Memorials.* Jefferson, N.C.: McFarland, 1988.

Works Progress Administration. *Federal Writers Program, Washington, D.C.,* New revised ed. New York: Hastings House, 1988.

Index